ESPECIALLY FOR

_____

FROM

_____

DATE

_____

Published by Barbour Publishing, Inc., P.O. Box 719, Uhrichsville, Ohio 44683, www.barbourbooks.com

Our mission is to publish and distribute inspirational products offering exceptional value and biblical encouragement to the masses.

Printed in China.

Life's Little Book of Encouragement for
teachers

BARBOUR
PUBLISHING

Be prepared in season and out of season;
correct, rebuke and encourage—
with great patience and careful instruction.

2 TIMOTHY 4:2 NIV

To awaken interest and kindle enthusiasm
is the sure way to teach easily and successfully.

Tyron Edwards

As a general rule, teachers teach more
by what they are than by what they say.

ANONYMOUS

The work can wait while you show the child the rainbow,
but the rainbow won't wait while you do the work.

PATRICIA CLAFFORD

kind words can be short and easy to speak,
but their echoes are endless.

MOTHER TERESA

The important thing is not so much that every child should be taught, as that every child should be given the wish to learn.

JOHN LUBBOCK

'Tis a lesson you should heed: Try, try, try again.
If at first you don't succeed, Try, try, try again.

W. E. HICKSON

A teacher is one who knows the way, goes the way, and shows the way.

J. C. Maxwell

My voice shalt thou hear in the morning,
O Lord; in the morning will I direct my prayer
unto thee, and will look up.

Psalm 5:3 KJV

Father, help me never forget the trust of a child is to be cherished.

Pamela Kay Tracy

It is the supreme art of the teacher to awaken joy
in creative expression and knowledge.

ALBERT EINSTEIN

Dear Jesus, help me not be so busy that
I miss the small pleasures You've sprinkled throughout
my day. . . . Give me a child's heart that sees
the lovely simple things in life.

ELLYN SANNA

He who asks a question is a fool for five minutes; he who does not ask a question remains a fool forever.

CHINESE PROVERB

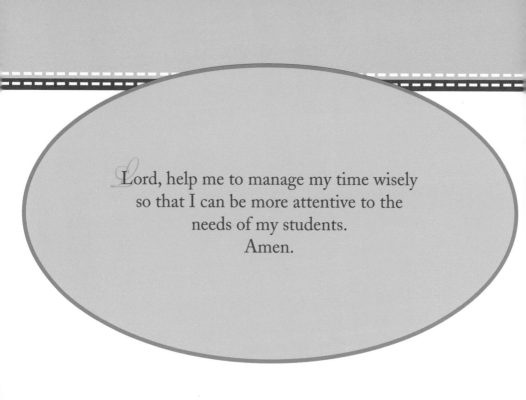

Lord, help me to manage my time wisely
so that I can be more attentive to the
needs of my students.
Amen.

Never have ideas about children—
and never have ideas for them.

D. H. LAWRENCE

When love and skill work together,
expect a masterpiece.

JOHN RUSKIN

But the temple the teacher built shall endure
while the ages roll; For that beautiful,
unseen temple was a child's immortal soul.

UNKNOWN

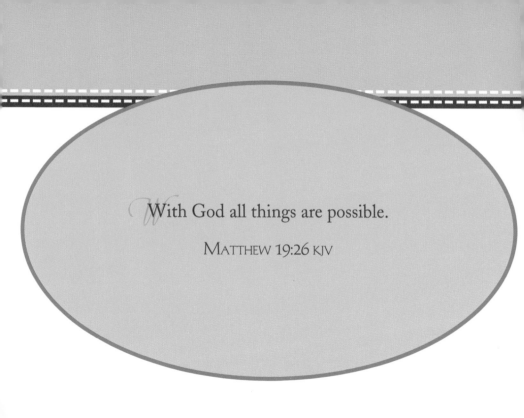

With God all things are possible.

MATTHEW 19:26 KJV

A man never stands as tall
as when he kneels to help a child.

ANONYMOUS

teaching should be full of ideas
instead of stuffed with facts.

UNKNOWN

Success is the sum of small efforts—
repeated day in and day out.

ROBERT COLLIER

Do what you love.

HENRY DAVID THOREAU

Your aspirations are your possibilities.

SAMUEL JOHNSON

the most important thing
about education is appetite.

Sir Winston Churchill

Father, when I have a student who is suffering,
show me ways to comfort him and somehow
lighten his load a little each day.
Amen.

to teach is to touch lives forever.

ANONYMOUS

In [Christ] are hidden all the treasures
of wisdom and knowledge.

COLOSSIANS 2:3 NIV

correction does much,
but encouragement does more.

JOHANN WOLFGANG VON GOETHE

When we long for life without difficulties,
remind us that oaks grow strong in contrary winds
and diamonds are made under pressure.

PETER MARSHALL

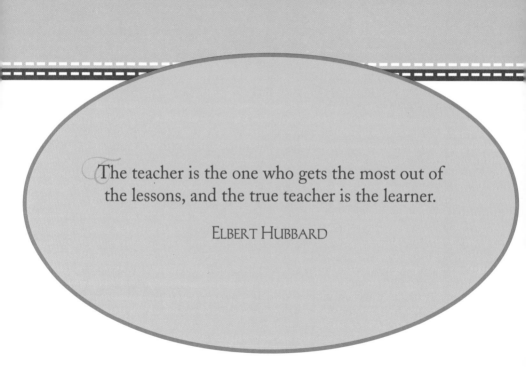

The teacher is the one who gets the most out of the lessons, and the true teacher is the learner.

ELBERT HUBBARD

successful people are not gifted; they just work hard and then succeed on purpose.

G. K. NIELSON

Here I am, Lord—body, heart, and soul.
Grant that with Your love, I may be big enough to reach
the world, and small enough to be at one with You.

MOTHER TERESA

Lord, help me to remember
the importance of the little things.

COLLEEN L. REECE AND ANITA CORRINE DONIHUE

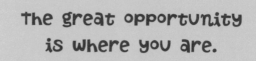

the great opportunity
is where you are.

JOHN BURROUGHS

What we see depends mainly
on what we look for.

JOHN LUBBOCK

And this I pray, that your love
may abound yet more and more in
knowledge and in all judgment.

PHILIPPIANS 1:9 KJV

teaching is the profession that
teaches all the other professions.

UNKNOWN

Your greatest pleasure is
that which rebounds from hearts
that you have made glad.

HENRY DAVID THOREAU

You gain strength, courage, and confidence by every experience in which you really stop to look fear in the face. You must do the thing that you think you cannot do.

Eleanor Roosevelt

Nothing is so strong as gentleness,
and nothing so great as real strength.

St. Francis de Sales

Learning is not attained by chance;
it must be sought for with ardor and diligence.

ABIGAIL ADAMS

Help me on sleepy, overcast days
to liven up my pupils' minds with colors of art
and the sounds of music and laughter.
Amen.

In what seems ordinary and everyday there is always more than at first meets the eye.

CHARLES CUMMINGS

The world of tomorrow belongs to the person
who has the vision for today.

ROBERT SCHULLER

Be strong in the grace that
is in christ jesus.

2 TIMOTHY 2:1 NIV

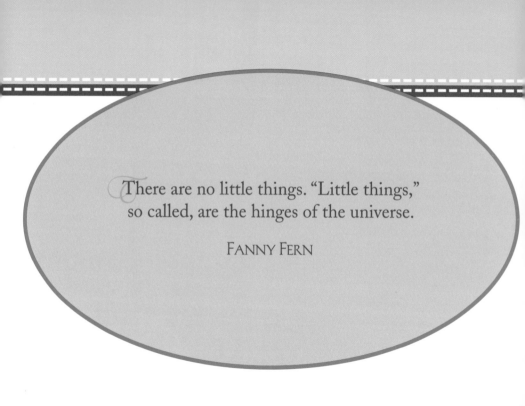

There are no little things. "Little things,"
so called, are the hinges of the universe.

FANNY FERN

praise does wonders for
the sense of hearing.

ANONYMOUS

Father, help me to keep my teaching fresh by approaching every day as if it were the first day of school.
Amen.

Whether sixty or sixteen, there is in every human being's heart the love of wonder, the sweet amazement at the stars and starlike things, the undaunted challenge of events, the unfailing childlike appetite for what-next, and the joy of the game of living.

SAMUEL ULLMAN

Education sows not seeds in you,
but makes your seeds grow.

KAHLIL GIBRAN

He that teaches us anything which we knew not before is undoubtedly to be reverenced as a master.

SAMUEL JOHNSON

How far you go in life depends on your being tender with the young, compassionate with the aged, sympathetic with the striving, and tolerant of the weak and the strong. Because someday in life you will have been all of these.

GEORGE WASHINGTON CARVER

what sculpture is to a block of marble,
education is to a human soul.

JOSEPH ADDISON

pleasant words are as an honeycomb,
sweet to the soul, and health to the bones.

PROVERBS 16:24 KJV

Tomorrow is a new day; begin it well and serenely and with too high a spirit to be cumbered with your old nonsense. This day is all that is good and fair. It is too dear, with its hopes and invitations, to waste a moment on yesterdays.

RALPH WALDO EMERSON

No pessimist ever discovered the secret to the stars, or sailed to an uncharted land, or opened a new doorway for the human spirit.

HELEN KELLER

When I am discouraged by the slow
progress I have made in my teaching, Lord,
instill in me fresh hope for tomorrow.
Amen.

Be patient with everyone, but above all with thyself.
I mean, do not be disheartened by your imperfections,
but always rise up with fresh courage.

ST. FRANCIS DE SALES

we must make the choices
that enable us to fulfill the deepest
capacities of ourselves.

THOMAS MERTON

Do the things at which you are great,
not what you were never made for.

RALPH WALDO EMERSON

Every day you shall wonder at yourself,
at the richness of life which has come
to you by the grace of God.

PHILLIPS BROOKS

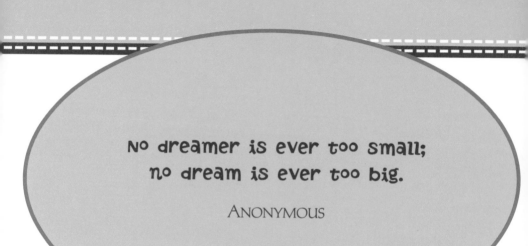

No dreamer is ever too small;
no dream is ever too big.

ANONYMOUS

You will rejoice, and no one will take away your joy.

JOHN 16:22 NIV

Everything that is full of life
loves change, for the characteristic of life
is movement toward a new goal.

Bishop Fulton Sheen

Rest is not idleness, and to lie sometimes on the grass
on a summer day listening to the murmur of water,
or watching the clouds float across the sky,
is hardly a waste of time.

JOHN LUBBOCK

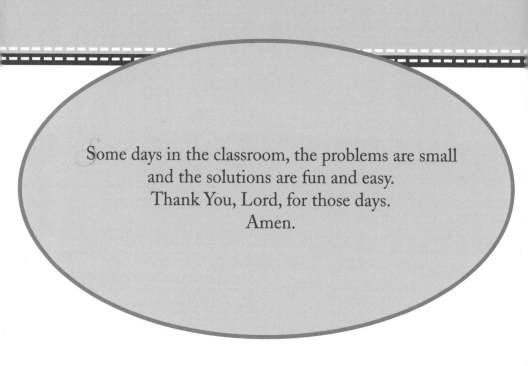

Some days in the classroom, the problems are small
and the solutions are fun and easy.
Thank You, Lord, for those days.
Amen.

You cannot discover new oceans unless you have the courage to lose sight of the shore.

UNKNOWN

The secret of genius is to carry the spirit of the child into old age, which means never losing your enthusiasm.

ALDOUS HUXLEY

You are sowing the flowers of tomorrow
in the seeds of today.

UNKNOWN

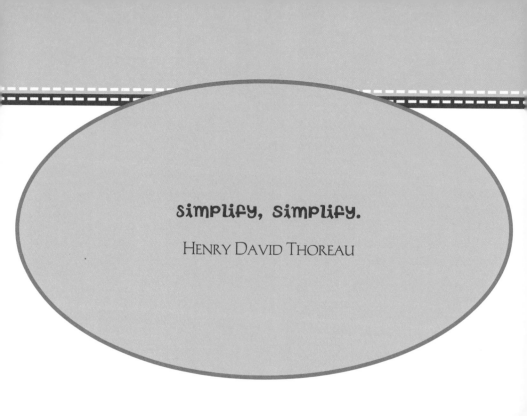

Simplify, Simplify.

HENRY DAVID THOREAU

The secret of joy in work is contained in one word— excellence. To know how to do something well is to enjoy it.

PEARL S. BUCK

And whatsoever ye do, do it heartily, as to the Lord, and not unto men.

COLOSSIANS 3:23 KJV

In ordinary life we hardly realize that we receive
a great deal more than we give, and that it
is only with gratitude that life becomes rich.

DIETRICH BONHOEFFER

Too often we underestimate the power of a touch, a smile, a kind word, a listening ear, an honest compliment, or the smallest act of caring, all of which have the potential to turn a life around.

LEO BUSCAGLIA

When I approach a child he inspires me
in two sentiments: tenderness for what he is,
and respect for what he may become.

LOUIS PASTEUR

Teachers who inspire know that teaching is like cultivating a garden, and those who would have nothing to do with thorns must never attempt to gather flowers.

UNKNOWN

wherever a man turns,
he can find someone who needs him.

ALBERT SCHWEITZER

The point is to develop the childlike inclination for play and the childlike desire for recognition and to guide the child over to important fields for society. Such a school demands from the teacher that he be a kind of artist in his province.

ALBERT EINSTEIN

Let me cherish busy days with
young people, happy to have a part in their world.
Help me to learn to slow down and relax in my teaching.
Amen.

Life is what we are alive to. It is not
length but breadth. . . . Be alive to. . .goodness,
kindness, purity, love, history, poetry, music,
flowers, stars, God, and eternal hope.

MALTBIE D. BABCOCK

I will instruct thee and teach thee
in the way which thou shalt go.

PSALM 32:8 KJV

We were not sent into this world to do anything into which we can not put our heart.

JOHN RUSKIN

we are what we repeatedly do. Excellence,
therefore, is not an act but a habit.

ARISTOTLE

The mind is not a vessel to be filled
but a fire to be ignited.

PLUTARCH

Be faithful in little things,
for in them our strength lies.

MOTHER TERESA

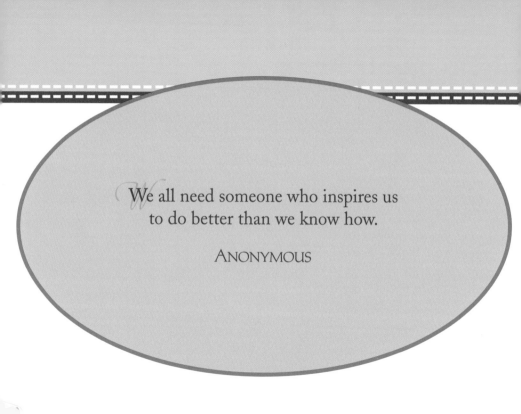

We all need someone who inspires us
to do better than we know how.

ANONYMOUS

A child's life is like a piece of paper
on which every passerby leaves a mark.

CHINESE PROVERB

To desire and strive to be of some service to the world,
to aim at doing something which shall really increase
the happiness and welfare and virtue of mankind—
this is a choice which is possible for all of us;
and surely it is a good haven to sail for.

HENRY VAN DYKE

Father, so many children come to school
hurting. Let me be a comfort in their lives.
Amen.

Incline thine ear unto wisdom,
and apply thine heart to understanding.

PROVERBS 2:2 KJV

Education is a companion
which no misfortune can depress, no crime can destroy,
no enemy can alienate, no despotism can enslave. . . .
Without it, what is man?

JOSEPH ADDISON

We find in life exactly what we put into it.

RALPH WALDO EMERSON

Goodness is the only investment
that never fails.

HENRY DAVID THOREAU

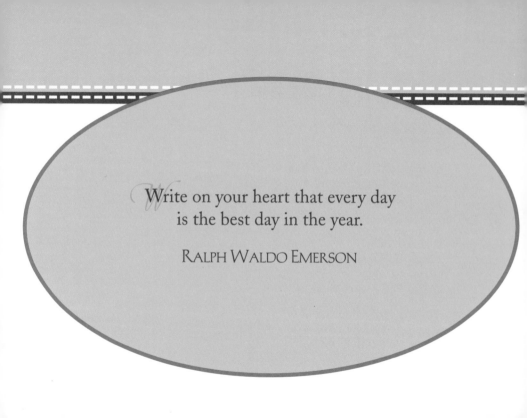

Write on your heart that every day
is the best day in the year.

RALPH WALDO EMERSON

A word of encouragement
during a failure is worth more than
an hour of praise after a success.

UNKNOWN

Lord, help me to give my students an unquenchable thirst for knowledge—
an ever-growing hunger for learning.
Amen.

the secret of education
is respecting the pupil.

RALPH WALDO EMERSON

children need models
rather than critics.

JOSEPH JOUBERT

A soft answer turneth away wrath:
but grievous words stir up anger.

Wonder is the desire for knowledge.

St. Thomas Aquinas

I am not a teacher, but an awakener.

ROBERT FROST

the teacher is one who makes two ideas grow where only one grew before.

ELBERT HUBBARD

Do not train children in learning by force and harshness,
but direct them to it by what amuses their minds,
so that you may be better able to discover with accuracy
the peculiar bent of the genius of each.

PLATO

To praise is an investment in happiness.

GEORGE M. ADAMS

A word fitly spoken is like apples
of gold in pictures of silver.

PROVERBS 25:11 KJV

when you have exhausted all possibilities,
remember this—you haven't.

THOMAS EDISON

$\mathcal{A}$ teacher who is attempting to teach
without inspiring the pupil with a desire
to learn is hammering on a cold iron.

HORACE MANN

Lord, I never know what student may be the
torch-carrier to future generations.
Help me to ignite a spark in each one.
Amen.

character may be manifested in the great
moments, but it is made in the small ones.

PHILLIPS BROOKS

when one door closes, another door opens.

ALEXANDER GRAHAM BELL

What makes the desert so beautiful
is that somewhere it hides a well.

ANTOINE DE SAINT-EXUPÉRY

A pessimist sees the difficulty in every opportunity;
an optimist sees the opportunity in every difficulty.

SIR WINSTON CHURCHILL

Everything that is done in this
world is done by hope.

MARTIN LUTHER

Teachers are the members of the most responsible, the least advertised, the worst paid, and the most richly rewarded profession in the world.

IAN HAY

Nothing great was ever achieved
without enthusiasm.

Ralph Waldo Emerson

the beginning is always today.

MARY WOLLSTONECRAFT

"Well done, good and faithful servant!"

MATTHEW 25:21 NIV

We cannot always build the future for our youth,
but we can build our youth for the future.

FRANKLIN D. ROOSEVELT

Vow to be valiant; resolve to be radiant; determine to be dynamic; strive to be sincere; aspire to be attuned.

WILLIAM ARTHUR WARD

Life's aspirations come in
the guise of children.

RABINDRANATH TAGORE

Thank You, Lord, for laughter and joy in my school day.
Thank You for a sense of humor and fun times.
Amen.

Do not go where the path may lead;
go instead where there is no path
and leave a trail.

RALPH WALDO EMERSON

The Constitution only gives people the right to pursue happiness. You have to catch it yourself.

BENJAMIN FRANKLIN

Wisdom is knowing what to do next.
Skill is knowing how to do it. Virtue is doing it.

THOMAS JEFFERSON

Resolve to see the world on the sunny side,
and you have almost won the battle of life at the outset.

SIR ROGER L'ESTRANGE

In everything set them an example by doing what is good. In your teaching show integrity, seriousness and soundness of speech that cannot be condemned.

TITUS 2:7-8 NIV

the really great man is the man
who makes every man feel great.

G. K. CHESTERTON

Do not let trifles disturb your tranquility of mind. . . .
Life is too precious to be sacrificed for
the nonessential and transient.

GLENVILLE KLEISER

the teacher is like the candle which
lights others in consuming itself.

ITALIAN PROVERB

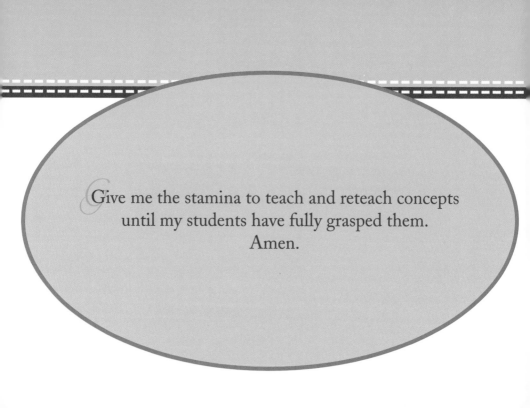

Give me the stamina to teach and reteach concepts until my students have fully grasped them.
Amen.

It is today that your best work can be
done and not some future day
or future year.

UNKNOWN

I find the great thing in this world is not so much where we stand as in what direction we are moving.

RALPH WALDO EMERSON

While we try to teach our children all about life,
our children teach us what life is all about.

ANONYMOUS

If a man does not keep pace with his companions, perhaps it is because he hears a different drummer. Let him step to the music which he hears, however measured or far away.

HENRY DAVID THOREAU

If it is serving, let him serve;
if it is teaching, let him teach.

ROMANS 12:7 NIV

I am indebted to. . .
my teacher for living well.

ALEXANDER THE GREAT

What we are is God's gift to us.
What we become is our gift to God.

ELEANOR POWELL

Cherish your visions; cherish your ideals; cherish the music that stirs in your heart, the beauty that forms in your mind, the loveliness that drapes your purest thoughts, for out of them will grow all delightful conditions, all heavenly environment.

JAMES ALLEN

Hover over my students, and if any need my help, let me be an approachable teacher. Amen.

Words so innocent and powerless as they are,
as standing in a dictionary, how potent. . .
they become in the hands of one who
knows how to combine them!

NATHANIEL HAWTHORNE

knowing is not enough; we must apply.
willing is not enough; we must do.

JOHANN WOLFGANG VON GOETHE

Use what talent you possess:
The world would be very silent if no birds
sang there except those that sang best.

HENRY VAN DYKE

Tell me and I forget. Show me and I remember.
Involve me and I understand.

CHINESE PROVERB

But remember the LORD your God, for it
is he who gives you the ability to produce wealth.

DEUTERONOMY 8:18 NIV

the main hope of a nation lies
in the proper education of its youth.

ERASMUS

More things are wrought by prayer
than this world dreams of.

ALFRED, LORD TENNYSON

Every heart that has beat strong and cheerfully has left a hopeful impulse behind it in the world and bettered the tradition of mankind.

ROBERT LOUIS STEVENSON

the heart is happiest when
it beats for others.

Dear God, save me from treading a
rut of my own making, and give me the desire
to bring freshness and new life to my work.

COLLEEN L. REECE AND ANITA CORRINE DONIHUE

Make the least ado about your greatest gifts.
Be content to act, and leave the talking to others.

BALTASAR GRACIAN

Learning is a treasure that
will follow its owner everywhere.

CHINESE PROVERB

Remind me daily, Lord, that as a teacher
what I say and do may stay with
these children for a lifetime.
Amen.

Example moves the world
more than doctrine.

HENRY MILLER

The Lord your God will make you abound in all the work of your hand.

Deuteronomy 30:9 NKJV

One day I would like to teach a few people
many wonderful and beautiful things that will help
them when they will one day teach a few people.

UNKNOWN

Yesterday is gone. Tomorrow has not come. We have only today. Let us begin.

MOTHER TERESA

There are two lasting bequests we can give our children:
One is roots, the other is wings.

ANONYMOUS

Father, may I never tire of planting seeds of learning in my students' minds that may someday produce abundant growth and a crop of wisdom and knowledge.
Amen.

Education is not the filling of a pail,
but the lighting of a fire.

WILLIAM BUTLER YEATS

A kind heart is a fountain of gladness, making everything in its vicinity freshen into smiles.

WASHINGTON IRVING

When you get into a tight place and everything goes against you, till it seems as though you could not hang on a minute longer, never give up then, for that is just the place and time that the tide will turn.

HARRIET BEECHER STOWE

Call unto me, and I will answer thee, and show thee great and mighty things, which thou knowest not.

JEREMIAH 33:3 KJV

*I*f you can bring one moment of happiness
into the life of a child, you are a coworker with God.

COLLEEN L. REECE AND ANITA CORRINE DONIHUE

Reflect upon your present blessings
of which every man has many; not on your past
misfortunes of which all men have some.

CHARLES DICKENS

Far away there in the sunshine are my
highest aspirations. I may not reach them, but
I can look up and see their beauty, believe in them,
and try to follow where they lead.

Louisa May Alcott

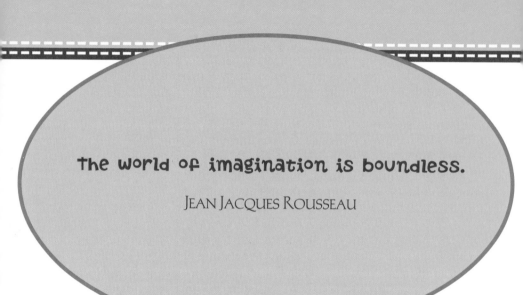

the world of imagination is boundless.

JEAN JACQUES ROUSSEAU

Hear instruction, and be wise, and refuse it not.

PROVERBS 8:33 KJV

A gentle word, a kind look, a good-natured smile
can work wonders and accomplish miracles.

WILLIAM HAZLITT

Do what you can,
with what you have, where you are.

THEODORE ROOSEVELT

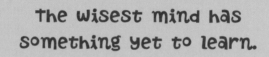

The wisest mind has
something yet to learn.

GEORGE SANTAYANA

A wise man will hear, and will increase learning;
and a man of understanding shall
attain unto wise counsels.

PROVERBS 1:5 KJV

Father, may we as teachers not only be instruments
in Thy hands, but shining tools You can
use for Your best purposes.

COLLEEN L. REECE AND ANITA CORRINE DONIHUE

May I be an example of kindness
and acceptance when a student joins us
who is handicapped or "different."
Amen.

Worlds can be found by a child and an adult bending down and looking together under the grass stems or at the skittering crabs in a tidal pool.

ANONYMOUS

O Divine Master, grant that I may not so much seek. . .
to be understood as to understand; to be loved as to love;
for it is in giving that we receive; it is in pardoning
that we are pardoned; and it is in dying that
we are born to eternal life.

Sᴛ. Fʀᴀɴᴄɪs ᴏғ Assɪsɪ

A teacher's purpose is not to create students in his own image, but to develop students who can create their own image.

UNKNOWN

Everyone has a unique role to fill in the world
and is important in some respect. Everyone, including
and perhaps especially you, is indispensable.

NATHANIEL HAWTHORNE

What we want is to see the child in pursuit of knowledge, and not the knowledge in pursuit of the child.

GEORGE BERNARD SHAW

It is the greatest of all mistakes to do nothing because you can only do a little. Do what you can.

SYDNEY SMITH

Trust in the LORD with all your heart and lean not on your own understanding; in all your ways acknowledge him, and he will make your paths straight.

PROVERBS 3:5-6 NIV

Great works are performed not by strength but by perseverance.

SAMUEL JOHNSON

God's grace keeps pace
with whatever we face.

UNKNOWN

Your heart is beating with God's love;
open it to others. He has entrusted you with gifts and
talents; use them for His service. He goes before you each
step of the way; walk in faith. Take courage. Step out
into the unknown with the One who knows all.

ELLYN SANNA

Dear Lord, help me to never be so busy
I fail to encourage, especially those who silently
cry out for my help and can do great things
if someone believes in them.

COLLEEN L. REECE AND ANITA CORRINE DONIHUE

The whole art of teaching is only
the art of awakening the natural curiosity of young
minds for the purpose of satisfying it afterwards.

ANATOLE FRANCE

the best teachers teach from
the heart, not from the book.

UNKNOWN

God understood our thirst for knowledge, and our need to be led by someone wiser; He needed a heart of compassion, of encouragement, and patience. . .someone who could see potential and believe in the best in others. . .so He made teachers.

UNKNOWN